My Role In The Local Church

"It's Ministry Time - Stay In Your Lane"

Copyright: This is the sole material of Joseph R. Rogers, Sr. and it is not to be copied or sold without written consent (cc: 2010)

Dr. Joseph R. Rogers, Sr.

Dedication

I would like to dedicate this writing to all Christian that are committed to the **Kingdom Work**, as you labor in the Ministry of our Lord Jesus Christ. I pray this information will enlighten, equip and energize your commitment to do local church ministry.

I have found that over the years that Leaders must prepare and qualify themselves as they go forth to serve others. You must remember that some ***saints*** drive for twenty minutes or more in traffic to hear what the Spirit has to say to the **"Church"**—they deserve the best teaching, worship and preaching!

I believe this is the reason the Lord has inspired me to accumulate and formulate this guide, that is, to help you ready yourself to meet the demands and challenges of today, as you go forth in Jesus name.

My aim, as directed by the Holy Ghost is to share with you *some simple* but *pertinent information* that is very practical and needed for our times. The body of Christ is precious because it was purchased by His precious blood.

In closing, it is my prayer that this book will serve you well and assist you in your Christian walk in the Lord. It will not cover every aspect of the local church functions, but I hope its contents will challenge you to better equip you for ministry.

God Bless,

Joseph R. Rogers, Sr.

Table Of Contents

	Page No.
Dedication	2
Introduction	6
I. The Pastor	8
II. The Assistant Pastor	16
III. The Associate Minister	19
IV. The Youth Pastor	24
V. The Youth Ministry President	31
VI. The Minister of Music	34
VII. The Musician	39
VIII. The Deacon	44
IX. The Men's Ministry Chairperson	50
X. The Women's Ministry Chairperson	55
XI. The Church Secretary	61
XII. The Church Clerk	68
XIII. The Church Treasurer	71

XIV. The Trustee--- 77

XV. The Financial Secretary----------------------------- 81

XVI. The Church School Superintendent--------------- 84

XVII. The Christian Education Director---------------- 88

XVIII. The Church Custodian---------------------------- 93

XIX. The Kitchen Ministry President/Chairperson--- 103

XX. The Floral Ministry President/Chairperson------- 106

XXI. The Ushers' Ministry President/Chairperson---- 109

XXII. The Evangelism Ministry President------------- 112

XXIII. The Outreach Ministry President-------------- 115

XXIV. The Hospitality President/Chairperson--------- 118

XXV. The Church Discipleship/Membership----------- 120

XXVI. Conclusion-- 128

XXVII. Contract Information & Other Works-------- 130

XXVIII. Notes-- 140

Introduction

Again, the Lord has encouraged my heart to share with my brothers and sisters some information that I believe will be an asset to your local church ministry.

The bible teaches us that whatsoever we do, it should be done **decent and in order and as unto the Lord".** This work is designed to equip you with the proper tools that it takes to equip, grow and mature your local church fellowship.

It is important that all programs and ministries within the local Church go forth under the unction and guidance of the Holy Ghost and that it be foundation upon the Word of God. This book will help you understand the function of groups, ministries, committees, chairpersons, presidents and other officers in your church.

The local congregation must not and should not be taken for granted when it comes to the leadership and its responsibilities. God's people deserve the best and those who stand before them should be at their **optimum mode of operation** at all times.

Over my thirty years of ministry I have had the opportunity to attend many local fellowships and services. Some have been excellent, while some have been poor. The difference has been ignorance, lack of proper training and lack of the understanding of biblical principles. **Traditions** have also caused great harm to the operation and growth of the local church.

God is a God of ***order, holiness, integrity and commitment*** and His church should possess His principles and mirror its actions after His. The Scriptures teaches us that when the Lord work, He move in decency and order—do the same!

So, with that said, it is my prayer that this book will help you, not only be better prepared, but also to help you understand the importance of order and proper protocol.

Peace, Grace & Blessings,

Joseph R. Rogers, Sr., D. Min.

I. SENIOR PASTOR

SCRIPTURAL PURPOSE: Hebrews 13:17; Jeremiah 3:15, 1 Peter 5:2

"Obey them that have the rule over you, and submit yourselves: for they watch for your souls, as they that must give account, that they may do it with joy, and not with grief: for that is unprofitable for you."

"And I will give you pastors according to mine heart, which shall feed you with knowledge and understanding.

"Feed the flock of God which is among you, taking the oversight thereof, not by constraint, but willingly; not for filthy lucre, but of a ready mind;"

A. THE ADMINISTRATIVE PURPOSE:

The Pastor of the Church of Jesus Christ is the highest positions in the kingdom of God. He/she is to be known as **SERVANT**. There is a tremendous responsibility that comes with this position, but there is also tremendous blessing that comes too.

The pastor has the awesome task of standing in the gap between God's desire/plan/vision for His people. The pastor has the responsibility of bringing the

Word of God to the congregation, so they can understand it. These instructions must include, but not limited to correction, direction, salvation, flavored with spirit of love.

The Pastor of the Church biblical has the responsibility of the general oversight of the church congregation. He/she must provide spiritual and pastoral care to the body of Christ.

At the same time, he/she must be able to provide administrative oversight, lead by example and serve as the visionary of the church.

He also has to lead the church in a positive direction; fulfilling the commands of the Bible. He/she should be a person of encouragement, prayer, and a leader in the study of the Word and yet, remain a practical person.

The Pastor is *"called"* of God and not chosen by the people. Ephesians 1:3 through 4 states, "Blessed be the God and Father of our Lord Jesus Christ, who hath blessed us with all spiritual blessings in heavenly places in Christ: According as he hath chosen us in him before the foundation of the world, that we should be holy and without blame before him in love:"

The Pastor of the Church must be opened minded with other leadership (deacons, elders) of the church, but he/she is responsible for carrying out the vision of God. He/she must be a great communicator. He/she must have the heart for the community in which he has been planted by the Lord.

B. PRIMARY RESPONSIBILITIES AND DUTIES:

SPIRITUAL: To Provide Spiritual Leadership First and Foremost In:

1. Prayer

A Pastor must be a man/woman of prayer. If the church is going to understand the power of God it will be through teaching them about prayer. A pastor must have the ability to call individuals to prayer, as well as the congregation. He/she must have an understanding of the power of prayer and fasting.

2. Preaching

A Pastor's obligation to the world is to preach the Gospel of Jesus Christ. They must understand the importance of sharing the knowledge of the Word, and cannot be swayed by public opinion. He/she will be held accountable for what he/she does with the preaching of the cross.

3. Administrate

A Pastor must administer communion, baptisms, weddings, funerals and baby dedications. He adds great blessings with dignity to the lives of those which Christ brings his/her way.

4. Leads

A Pastor leads the congregation into a deep trust, love and obedience to Jesus Christ. Not only must he/she lead in word, but it must also be by example.

5. Keeps the Peace

A Pastor must be able to keep peace, in the body of Christ, among the church members. The scripture is very clear when it come to the temperament of leadership. It must be under control.

B. ADMINISTRATIVE:

a. To be a great strategic leader he/she must be able to coordinate staff in the process of capturing the Lord's vision for the local congregation.

b. To oversee the training of leadership within the church and make sure it stays in agreement with the bible. He/she must be able to administrate the needs of the church such as, hospital visits, family visits and meetings by coordinating the staff and delegating of authority.

c. He/she is chairperson of the church business meetings and must lead the staff to develop church programs that will help build stable, committed, Christian people.

C. GENERAL QUALIFICATIONS:

1. They must have the heart of a pastor, a man/woman after God's heart. They must be wise, caring, gentle and maintain a personal study time, prayer life, continual reading and learning of God's Word, so as to fulfill God's purpose and will for his life.

2. They must be effective in communication skills. They must be able to bring understanding to the Word, and then sit in an administrative meeting and discuss business, insurance, accounting and all the practical needs of the church; with understanding and the ability to lead the meeting or delegate as he sees fit.

3. They must keep privacy and confidentiality as the absolute trust of his position. He must make sure notes and journals are kept private, during counseling sessions, and no one, other than the authorized people to handle that information, are able to get it for any

reasons. His office dictates complete privacy and confidentiality.

4. They must be a great discerner of people, character and be willing to listen to the counsel of their staff for safe leadership. He/she must hold dear the verse that states, **"There is safety in the counsel of the godly."**

D. DUTIES TO HANDLE THE STRATEGIC NEEDS OF THE CHURCH:

1. They must give primary supervision to all the departments of the church operations. The pastor is to act as chairperson to all departments and ministries.

2. They must define job descriptions and make sure people hired meet job skill expectations and are in agreement with the church vision.

3. They must be able to communicate feedback in a kind and gentle manner, not being critical or demanding.

4. They must hold weekly meetings and or as deemed necessary. When organization meet as need all lines of communication will not become clogged with unnecessary chatter.

5. They must keep regular and posted hours of availability to the congregation. The pastor must take time to minister to the congregation.

6. They must make the primary decisions for the church after consulting God through sincere prayer.

7. They must protect the reputation of the perceived role of a pastor, the finances of the church and maintain moral and ethical purity.

E. SUMMARY:

What an amazing, wonderful and powerful position a pastor has. He/she is underneath or subject to Jesus Christ as the leader, shepherd, teacher, doctor, caregiver, or said in a much simplier way, *"all things to all men"* in the body of Christ. He/she get joy in fulfilling that vision that God has given him/her. He/she encourages and nurtures the spiritual development of people and leads them into a deeper and abiding life in Christ.

The participation in the growth of fellowship and the mentoring of fine young men and women is what pastoring is all about. Pastors are able to provide counsel, share the heartbeat of God, with others, and see the power of God working in their midst.

The power of God can be seen clearly in a man/woman that walks with integrity, honesty and moral uprightness. Living a life that glorifies God is a powerful position of influence. It should never be used selfishly.

II. ASSISTANT PASTOR

SCRIPTURAL PURPOSE: Exodus 4:27-30

"And the Lord said to Aaron, Go into the wilderness to meet Moses. And he went, and met him in the mount of God, and kissed him. And Moses told Aaron all the words of the Lord who had sent him, and all the signs which he had commanded him. And Moses and Aaron went and gathered together all the elders of the children of Israel: And Aaron spake all the words which the Lord had spoken unto Moses, and did the signs in the sight of the people."

A. ADMINISTRATIVE PURPOSE:

The Assistant Pastor is an extremely intimate, partner position to the pastor. It is a position that agrees completely with the vision and the fulfillment of the pastor. This is in no way is saying that when it come to administration, the Assistant Pastor has to be a puppet, rubber stamp or without an opinion. The Assistant Pastor must offer the pastor backbone, but at the same time, understand that he/she is not the senior pastor of the church.

The Assistant Pastor must be able to administrator "in place of" the Pastor if called upon to do so. He/she should have the same zeal as the senior pastor for the Lord and have the ability to carry the burdens of the Senior Pastor if needed to do so. His duties are pretty much summed up in that he performs the same duties of the called and ordained pastor.

By the very nature of the job description, he is authorized and obligated to work in unity with the Senior Pastor.

B. PRIMARY RESPONSIBILITIES AND DUTIES:

1. Preach and teach with authority.

2. Discharge the functions as delegate by the senior pastor

3. Guard and guide the congregation at the call of the senior pastor

4. Meet regularly with the Senior Pastor and become a cherished friend and confidante.

5. Be able to make sound decisions within the operations of the church environment, not with consulting the senior pastor.

6. Serve the congregation in love and demonstration of the Holy Spirit.

C. GENERAL QUALIFICATIONS:

1. A degree in Theology and or Ministry.

2. Ordained minister.

3. Relevant experience that demonstrates the call of God clearly.

D. SUMMARY:

The Assistant Pastor, like Aaron with Moses, is a truly in an intimate and caring position. There are some relationships in the Bible that show the love and the expertise the Senior Pastor and the Assistant Pastor should have.

As way of example, the first being **Aaron and Moses**, the second **David and Jonathan**, the third, **Jesus and his disciples**, and fourth The Apostle **Paul and Timothy**. This is a position where learning, expanding of the ministry and depending on the Lord and each other grows daily.

This servant must be a person of integrity, loyalty, submission, prayer and confidentiality. It is a position past the concept of friend or associate to one of fellow *"Servant"* in the Lord.

III. ASSOCIATE MINISTER

SCRIPTURAL PURPOSE: Act 15:22, 1 Timothy 1:18

"Then pleased it the apostles and elders with the whole church, to send chosen men of their own company to Antioch with Paul and Barnabas; namely, Judas surnamed Barsabas and Silas, chief men among the brethren:"

"This charge I commit unto thee, son Timothy, according to the prophecies which went before on thee, that thou by them mightiest war a good warfare;"

A. ADMINISTRATIVE PURPOSE:

The Associate Minister is a position that really ***"fills in" or "helps"*** the Senior Pastor. Often times he/she is placed within a specific area of need within the church. They fill the needs in the administrative, youth, education, adult ministry and basically any department at the request of the senior pastor.

The Associate Minister as the Assistant Pastor must at no time attempt to assume the role of senior pastor at his or her call—these positions even though they have responsibilities; yet they have no senior pastoral authority.

The Associate Minister must develop relationships of trust and keep in agreement with the Senior Pastor, according to the vision he is implement-ting within the congregation.

They must be able to motivate people and show enthusiasm for the work of the Lord. He/she must be supportive of the vision, policies and ministries of the church. He/she must possess a positive spirit, and be a person that has a strong work ethic. He/she must be a team player.

B. PRIMARY RESPONSIBILITIES AND DUTIES:

*Proclaim the Gospel through preaching, teaching or helps in the departments they might be placed to minister.

*Provide emergency response in crisis situations to relieve the Senior Pastor.

*Teach, mentor and oversee committees at the senior pastor's appointing.

* Develop challenging, but achievable goals for themselves and the congregation.

*They must be able to make sound decisions within the operations of the church environment.

*Reach the community and find opportunities to create outreach evangelism programs.

C. General Duties that are Pastoral:

1. Pastoral: Worship, Preaching, Baptisms, Weddings, Funerals Counseling.

2. Evangelism: Visitations.

3. Administration: Staff meetings and Congregational meetings.

4. Education: Coordinate and Train leaders in Sunday school, Youth and Adult ministries.

5. New Members: Create plans and programs for new members to blend into the congregation quickly.

6. Team Ministry: Support the Vision.

7. Accountability: To the Senior Pastor.

D. GENERAL QUALIFICATIONS

1. A degree in Theology or Ministry
2. Ordained minister.
3. Relevant experience that demonstrates the call of God clearly.

E. DESIRED PERSONAL QUALIFICATIONS:

1. They must be a man/woman of prayer and Bible study.
2. They must live a life of high moral and spiritual integrity.
3. They must demonstrate an ability to manage ministry.
4. They must be in agreement with the basic doctrines of the church.
5. They must have knowledge and be experienced to work within the congregation.
6. They must maintain the ability to care for the lost, hurting, elderly and youth.

7. They must meet the scriptural commands of elder leadership in II Timothy 3: 1-17.

F. SUMMARY:

The Associate Minister is an encourager, under girder and helps the pastor, the staff, the congregation and the community. The way they perform their duties helps to unify the body and the flow of the Holy Spirit. Through their gift of fellowship and prayer this ministry is important in the church's growth and stability.

The Associate Minister must not be a striver or argumentative, but must fulfill the office wearing many hats. He/she is instrumental to the organizational and spiritual growth of the congregation, as well as to relieving the Senior Pastor of extra burdens. In the end he is a servant to the Servant of the Lord.

IV. YOUTH PASTOR

SCRIPTURAL PURPOSE: Ecclesiastes 11: 9a; 12:1, 13

"Rejoice, O young man, in thy youth; and let thy heart cheer thee in the days of thy youth,"

"REMEMBER now thy Creator in the days of thy youth, while the evil days come not, nor the years draw nigh, when thou shalt say, I have no pleasure in them;"

"Let us hear the conclusion of the whole matter: Fear God, and keep his commandments: for this is the whole duty of man."

A. ADMINISTRATIVE PURPOSE:

Realizing that young people are an important and vital part of the church and the community, Youth Pastors must be serious about their relationship with God in Jesus Christ, and present that relationship to those he or she is trying to reach.

The Youth Pastor must have a firm grasp of Scripture and an active prayer life. Being able to speak challenging words to youth, and sometimes parents, is part of the ministry that can be challenging at times, but must never be argumentative.

The Youth Pastor must have a real connection to church life; including the doctrines of the church, its moral teachings and the ability to love and care for the youth of the church and the community. The main character trait necessary for service is a real desire to serve. They basically are evangelist who live and preach the gospel with joy and conviction before the youth and families of the church and the community.

The Youth Pastor must know how to set boundaries, while at the same time being a mentor, an example, a teacher and at all times a real friend. The spiritual and the social needs of youth and family are to be met with consistent leadership and support.

The Youth Pastor must be passionate about justice and peace as well as fostering church teaching on respecting life at all its stages and circumstances. The Youth Pastor must be a team player and work with the group to assure the vision, direction, planning and implementation of the youth ministry programs are in line with the pastoral vision and the mission of the Church.

B. ACCOUNTABILITY TO:

Senior Pastor

* Will meet at least once a week and lay out the evaluation, direction, support and agenda of the youth ministries.

* Will be prepared to give a summary of ministry to the church ministries meetings, as asked to.

* Will keep accurate financial records of spending on youth ministry expenses.

C. PERSONAL ATTRIBUTES OF A YOUTH PASTOR:

A. Personal Relationship with Christ

a) They must have a personal life of worship.

b) Continuing education to keep current with events, news, church conventions for youth, classes and self-improvement.

c) Must be willing to have friends they will be accountable to that will keep the "tool sharp."

d) Must be a role model, and have a loyalty to the church and the community in which they will be working in.

e) Maintain a strong and healthy relationship with their family.

f) Willing to share their faith in Jesus openly and strongly.

g) Personal love and commitment for young people.

C. PRIMARY RESPONSIBILITIES AND DUTIES:

1. They must have a well prepared plan and be able to reach the community and the church with outreach programs and helps ministry.

2. They should try to meet the leaders of the city, schools, businesses and churches to maintain positive relationships.

3. They should lead youth into strong spiritual disciplines for their own life. They should teach them about devotionals, daily reading of Scripture and faithful attendance of church functions and services.

4. They must be an exceptional communicator to all age groups.

5. They must meet the qualifications set forth in I Timothy 3:1-7.

6. They must be willing to work with primary care givers or parents in social and state requirements.

7. They must take a course on Sexual Harassment and make guidelines for the youth team and youth group.

D. GENERAL QUALIFICATIONS:

1. Must have zeal and love for the Lord, and be able to express it openly.

2. Must be a good leader and delegator. They must not try to "DO IT ALL."

3. Must have fresh ideas and be creative.

4. Must be enthusiastic, prepared and ready to guide and teach the youth.

E. DUTIES OF YOUTH MINISTRY LEADERSHIP TEAM:

1. They must attend monthly leadership meetings.

2. They must serve on the planning programs.

3. They must attend, be active in and minister to youth at all planned activities.

4. They must provide support for children's needs and visit the families of the youth.

5. They must maintain a proper code of conduct at all times.

6. They must report anything that would be considered suspect or illegal.

7. They must maintain records for stewardship campaigns.

8. They must perform any tasks requested by the Finance Committee, Pastor or Board.

F. SUMMARY:

The Youth Pastor must have a clear understanding of discipline, love, care-giving and spiritual nurturing. They must walk a very fine line at times, and so they must stay informed as to the laws and regulations, when dealing with youth.

The Youth Pastor must be "The Example" that a lot of youth never have the opportunity to see. They must be a leader, mentor and spiritual advisor.

The Youth Pastor must be comfortable with the dynamics of the differences found in different cultures, beliefs and basically the family unit. They must have a faith-focused message. They must strengthen the family relationships, as well as bring the family into the congregation as members of the church.

The Youth Pastor must care, serve and be available spiritually and physically. They have a position of "standing in the gap" between the lost, within the city, and the place of refuge, the church.

V. YOUTH MINISTRY PRESIDENT

SCRIPTURAL PURPOSE: I Timothy 1:18, 19

"This charge I commit unto thee, son Timothy, according to the prophecies which went before on thee, that thou by them mightiest war a good warfare; Holding faith, and a good conscience; which some having put away concerning faith have made shipwreck:"

A. ADMINISTRATIVE PURPOSE:

The Youth Ministry President has an obligation to bring the youth of the church and the community into a mature, abiding and lasting faith in Jesus Christ.

Through the organization of different departments, missions and activities it is their duty to bring a cohesive group of young people together to begin to learn how to operate in their gifts and callings with balance.

The Youth Ministry President should plan rallies, camps, websites and use different tools to reach a younger age group, than the church possibly does in a Sunday morning service. They should study to show themselves approved and be seen as mature and complete in the Lord, as an example to youth.

B. PRIMARY RESPONSIBILITIES AND DUTIES:

They must foster a cohesive youth group based on the Scriptures and coordinate different functions, to reach out to youth that are not part of the core group.

1. They must develop strategies to increase the body of Christ.
2. They must provide training for youth.
3. They should be able to identify opportunities, within the schools and city, to motivate youth to a new walk in Jesus Christ.

C. GENERAL QUALIFICATIONS:

1. They must be full of energy and have a tremendous love for the Lord and youth.

2. They must be a good communicator, planner and authority figure.

3. They must have a submissive heart, to church leadership, and be a team player.

D. SUMMARY:

The Youth Ministry President is a position of great influence for the youth of the church. They can organize a great work force, missions group, Bible study class.

Young People have a natural zeal to want to be productive and with a great youth president who can motivate and teach is a vital asset. A good youth president and a great group of young people are necessary to maintain steady church growth and balance in the life of a church fellowship.

VI. MINISTER OF MUSIC

SCRIPTURAL PURPOSE: I Chronicles 16:29, Psalm 95:1

"Give unto the Lord the glory due unto his name: bring an offering, and come before him: worship the Lord in the beauty of holiness."

"O come, let us sing unto the LORD: let us make a joyful noise to the rock of our salvation"

A. ADMINISTRATIVE PURPOSE:

The Minister of Music must be a mature believer and is responsible for organizing, conducting and evaluating the worship style and performance within the Church.

The Minister of Music must have an education in music, a college degree or at least the demonstration of excellence with music, musicians, voice and organizational skills. They should have a heart of worship, and be able to display that worship to the congregation.

The Minister of Music should have the ability to bring the congregation into a place of praise and worship in every service they are called upon to serve in.

The Minister of Music must have exceptional leadership skills in the area of dealing with the congregation and moving them to a place of participation, not just observation.

The Minister of Music is an important position. The Worship attitude of the congregation sets the atmosphere for receiving the power of Holy Spirit, as the pastor preaches. The Minister of Music is the director of all church music, is subordinate to the senior pastor.

The Minster of Music must be able to plan and carry out the musical programs of the church. They must also have a dynamic teaching and training ability; in order to keep the church well supplied with singers and musicians. It is not enough to be talented and gifted; the Music Director must be affirmed by the Holy Spirit with fruit that can be judged. They must exhibit a character deeply committed to God, the call of God and the placement of God into the body of Christ.

B. REQUIREMENTS:

1. A college or seminary degree first; at least a high school diploma, if the exceptional skills are visible; or at least a minimum of one year of leading worship.

2. They must be computer literate: Microsoft Word and Power Point...etc.

3. They must be in good health. They will be required to walk, stand and sit, sometimes for very prolonged periods of time, during a service.

4. They must have great communication skills and work well with others.

5. They must pass criminal, financial and sexual misconduct background checks.

6. They must be able to lead and accompany worship services.

7. They must organize, audition, rehearse and coordinate the worship teams.

8. They must maintain a music library by selecting and organizing different songs, plays and worship materials.

9. They must select and coordinate any "Special Music" presentations.

10. They must select musicians for all services, all choir members and work with practice workshops for those wanting to join the choir or musicians ranks.

11. They will answer to the Senior Pastor

12. They will oversee and coordinate music for special events such as Easter, Christmas and Thanksgiving.

13. They will oversee lyric displays for the services.

14. They will lead the congregational singing.

15. They will be aware of wedding and funeral music needs within the church.

C. MUSICAL BACKGROUND:

A. They should have the ability to read and direct music.

B. They must have an ability to sing and play a musical instrument.

C. They must lead worship without hesitation or shyness.

D. They must have a strong knowledge with contemporary Christian music, as well as the old church hymns.

E. They must have a calling for the music ministry and be a born again believer of The Lord Jesus Christ.

F. They must be able to supervise and coordinate the work.

D. SUMMARY:

The Minister of Music is accountable to the pastor, and is one of the most important positions of leadership within the church. People come to church for many different reasons and some are heavy hearted.

Music plays an important role in helping the person leave the **"real world"** for a short period of time to enter into the worship of the King of Kings. Worship should be powerful, but effective, forceful and yet full of peace. It should bring a person to the throne room of God and He in turns ministers to them or meet them at the point of their needs.

VII. MUSICIAN

SCRIPTURAL PURPOSE: II Chronicles 5:13, 14

"It came even to pass, as the trumpeters and singers were as one, to make one sound to be heard in praising and thanking the Lord; and when they lifted up their voice with the trumpets and cymbals and instruments of musick, and praised the Lord, saying, For he is good; for his mercy endureth for ever: that then the house was filled with a cloud, even the house of the Lord; So that the priest could not stand to minister by reason of the cloud: for the glory of the Lord had filled the house of God."

A. ADMINISTRATIVE PURPOSE:

The Musician sole function is to produce music for the worship of the Lord during the congregational service times. Most musicians are professionals in one or two instruments and have an **"inner"** understanding of how to flow in the emotion or heartbeat of the music to be played.

The Musician can be a soloist or even be expected to play in a group setting. They must be accountable to Minister of Music and the choirs by practicing the music material and being loyal by showing up on time and performing to the best of their abilities under the anointing of the Holy Spirit.

The **Musicians** have been blessed with a talent that those of us, who don't have that gift, find fascinating. All anointed musician are gifted at birth, but must enhance their ministry through some studies in the music discipline which will fine tune their God gifted abilities (remember practice make perfect).

The Musician must be able to sit under the leadership of the Music Director and the Pastor, and yet have the unique ability to interpret music without overstepping the leader's authority or direction. The Minister of Music or the Musician is not the Shepherd (Pastor) of the flock and must never ever try to be. The Pastor is the Chief Worship Leader and Chief Education Director.

B. PRIMARY RESPONSIBILITIES AND DUTIES:

1. They must play appropriately the music that the Music Director and or Pastor have chosen for the morning and evening worship services, as well as other requested services.

2. They must be agreeable to accompany choirs and soloists in a background position when needed.

3. They must be willing to be a substitute, in case someone fails to show up.

4. They should have a working knowledge of software technology as; it pertains to their talent (i.e. taps, cd's and dvd's)

5. They must attend any meetings, rehearsals or requests of the Music Director. The Musician must be a born again believer in the Lord Jesus Christ.

C. GENERAL QUALIFICATIONS:

1. They must have a discernable talent that can be seen and heard readily.

2. They must have a cooperative spirit.

3. They must have a strong performance style.

4. They must be able to accompany in different capacities the needs of the director.

5. They must yield to the director's leading, and still be led of the Holy Spirit.

D. SPECIAL DUTIES

1. They must perform in public.

2. They must practice outside of the demands the church requires of them.

3. They must maintain their instrument and set-up equipment before services (or direct others to do the same)

4. They must attend rehearsals and be on time. It would be good for the Music Director and Musician to arrive early to outline what will be practiced before the choir arrives.

D. Summary

The Musician is a vital piece to the puzzle of church worship. They play an integral part necessary to the performance of the music, at the level of excellence, it was meant to be heard. They usually have several jobs at different locations, in order to make their living as a musician. It is extremely important to understand the demands that are put on their time schedules and how valuable their time is.

The Musician that use his/her talents for the Lord allow the congregation to experience all levels of worship from praise, to prophecy, to worship or just listening to the sound the Spirit of God brings through their instruments to quiet the soul.

When David played the harp Saul's angry spirit was quieted. A musician can set the atmosphere of the service, and if surrendered and humble can allow the Holy Spirit to come and move among the people ministering to the unspoken needs deep within their hearts.

VIII. DEACON

SCRIPTURAL PURPOSE: Acts 6:2,3

"Then the twelve called the multitude of the disciples unto them, and said, it is not reason that we should leave the word of God, and serve tables". Wherefore, brethren, look ye out among you seven men of honest report, full of the Holy Ghost and wisdom, whom we may appoint over this business."

A. ADMINISTRATIVE PURPOSE:

1. The Deacon is a person who has some very specific qualifications.

2. The Deacon have been called out of the body of Christ (local) to assist the senior pastor and helpful in maintaining spirituality, unity, morality and dignity within the church fellowship

3. Deacons are to be honest.

4. Deacons are to be full of the Holy Ghost.

5. The Deacon must also have wisdom.

6. The Deacons are called to work in practical realms within the church, but be assured their task is spiritual.

7. The Deacons are under the oversight of elders and pastors of the church. I Timothy 3:8-13 it clearly states, that a deacon must be tested before he can serve in this leadership role.

8. The Deacons must be an example to others by their character and gifts to the body of Christ. And they share in the affairs of the church; working to help others and allowing pastors to be relieved of the everyday pressures of ministry.

B. PRIMARY RESPONSIBILITIES:

The first and primary duty of the Deacon is to be a person who is faithful to their family and leads their family into daily prayer, reading of God's Word and praise.

1. The Deacons must set the example of a godly family, so that others can learn from them and follow in the same pattern or manner. They are to set their spiritual gifts in the service of their family first, and then to the congregation.

2. The Deacon must be faithful, abiding members of the church and to take on the temporal affairs of the church.

3. The Deacon should assist in the Lord's Supper distribution and with ushering duties.

4. The Deacon must be willing to work with the pastor in matters of discipline within the church.

5. The Deacon must be sound in Word and doctrine.

6. The Deacon must perform the duties of the outreach ministries of the church, such as the feeding of the poor.

C. GENERAL QUALIFICATIONS: I Timothy 3:7-14

1. They must be grave/sober, not double tongued, not given too much wine, not greedy of filthy lucre.

2. They must teach the pure and sound word of God holding the mystery of the faith in a pure conscience.

3. They must be mature in faith, not a novice.

4. They must have a good reputation.

5. They must be the husband of one wife.

6. Wives must have a good reputation.

7. They must be in control of his or her household.

8. They must be known for their faith in the community.

9. In Titus 1:5: They must be an organizer.

10. In Acts 20:28-31: They must be able to defend the body of Christ from false teachers.

D. DUTIES TO HANDLE THE STRATEGIC NEEDS OF THE CHURCH:

1. They must give service help to all the departments of the church's operations.

2. They are to work closely with church leadership.

3. They must labor in the Word and teach sound doctrine.

4. They must assist leadership in disciplinary matters when called upon.

5. They must work diligently, with the church, to reach out to the Underprivileged.

6 . They must equip the saints to maturity. (Ephesians 4:11-15)

7. They lead by example.

8. They must be willing to be enlisted on church committees as needed or requested.

E. SUMMARY:

The Deacon starts his service to the Lord in his own house first! They are leaders, humble servants and they secure the knowledge of the Lord in their families first.

*They are ministers of prayer to their own families.

* They are known in the community as people of faith.

*They live what they preach. They are examples of righteousness and integrity.

*They show the world that it is possible to be a man or woman of God.

*They are to have proven character.

*They are to have a reputation.

The Deacons are not to be moved by circumstances, but as Scripture states they are honest, full of the Holy Spirit and overflow with wisdom.

The Deacons should be able to tackle problems and bring quick solutions, because God has given them that ability. In other words, the deacons must put out all fires and babblings in the church fellowship.

IX. MEN'S MINISTRY CHAIRPERSON

SCRIPTURAL PURPOSE: Proverbs 3:13

"Blessed is the man who finds wisdom, the man who gains understanding."

A. ADMINISTRATIVE PURPOSE:

The Men's Ministry Chairperson is to serve by developing a work that meets the needs of men to help them learn how to pursue God. They are to form a vital men's ministry by working with men in the local church and the community.

The Men's Ministry Chairperson must reach out and let men know they are not alone in this world. The Men's Ministry Chairperson should actively pursue men and get them acquainted with the Word of God, and challenge men to go deeper into a committed walk with God and their families.

Scripture states, "The man of integrity walks securely..." Thus the Men's Chairperson must be a person who has a deep, mature, Christ-like faith and lifestyle. He must be an example that men can look up to and respect as he teaches them to have a deeper relationship with Christ.

B. PRIMARY RESPONSIBILITIES AND DUTIES:

The Men's Ministry Chairperson should be able to develop and coordinate men's Bible study groups.

** **The Men's Ministry Chairperson** should be a great motivator calling men into leadership positions and training them how to duplicate the program with others.

The growth of men spiritually is the main emphasis of men's ministry. He should be able to teach and mentor men in all areas of spiritual life such as, prayer, devotions, Bible study, parenting, spouse support, business and community service.

The Men's Ministry Chairperson should be able to develop programs for men with needs in addictive behaviors.

The Men's Ministry Chairperson should be able to provide counseling or direct men for counsel when needed.

The Men's Ministry Chairperson should be able to teach men how to be the spiritual leaders of their families by love and not domination.

**The Men's Ministry Chairperson must, in his own personal life, be the example of the servant of the Lord.

**The Men's Ministry Chairperson must develop programs that bring men together for fellowship, service and spiritual growth. The end result should be men that are true disciples of Jesus Christ.

C. GENERAL QUALIFICATIONS:

1. A man of love and prayer.

2. Great organizational skills.

3. A heart of a servant.

D. DUTIES TO HANDLE THE NEEDS OF MEN:

1. Fellowship among the brethren. This calls for luncheons, breakfasts, Bible studies, etc.

2. Training programs to help men grow spiritually.

3. Reaching out to other men is an essential part of men's ministries.

4. Sharing their faith as the end result of sound training.

5. Resisting temptation becomes easier when a group of men are a band of brothers.

6. Making a difference in the church, home, and community.

7. Praying together to create a powerful bond seeing the hand of God move in their midst.

F. SUMMARY:

The Men's Ministry Chairperson is vital to the health and blessing of the families in the church. He directs everything he does, says, provides and plans to help men grow deeper into a holy and special relationship with Jesus Christ.

The activity of the church and the enjoyment of the church functions can often be traced to the men's ministry. Men leading with a prayerful, active and servant's heart can make the families of a church continue to mature and be blessed.

Well trained men, in the service of the Lord, can become the underlying security the church needs to be healthy and vital to the community. Godly men are needed, wanted, appreciated and loved.

The Men's Ministry Chairperson is to surrender his life for the sake of others. This action will be the call to other men desiring to go higher in their spiritual lives.

X. WOMAN'S MINISTRY CHAIRPERSON

SCRIPTURAL PURPOSE: Proverbs 31:10

"Who can find a virtuous woman? For her price is far above rubies."

A. ADMINISTRATIVE PURPOSE:

The Women's Ministry Chairperson has probably one of the most influential job roles within the church. Women are vital to the operation of the ministry and the creation of healthy families that become part of the body of Christ.

The Women's Ministry Chairperson are called to assist in the various spiritual, emotional, financial, parenting and intellectual needs of women, not just within the church (although that is the first priority), but within the community as well.

The Women's Ministry Chairperson must not only meet the various needs of women, they must also be exceptional leaders and show great organizational and communication skills. The Bible gives us great insight to many different women, and what they have accomplished.

The main point to be considered with women, thus the main objective of women's ministry, is that Jesus ministered to women and he always restored their self-worth and value as human beings.

There is probably no greater work within the church than women's ministries. When women are ministered to the church, the family and the community benefit.

B. PRIMARY RESPONSIBILITIES AND DUTIES:

**She should be able to develop and coordinate women's Bible study groups.

** She should have a compassionate, caring nature and understand a clear, spiritual purpose for God's plan for women in today's world.

**She assists the church in keeping the women's ministry meeting the spiritual and practical base of operations within the church.

**She should be able to develop programs for women with needs in a diverse number of areas.

** She should be able to provide counseling for women as needed.

**She should be able to teach women how to live balanced lives with their families; by love not domination.

**She must be the example of a Godly woman in every area of her life.

**She must develop programs that bring women together for fellowship, service and spiritual growth. The end result should be women that are true disciples of Jesus Christ.

C. GENERAL QUALIFICATIONS:

1. A woman of love, prayer, service and balance.

2. Great organizational and communication skills.

3. The heart of a servant who is sensitive, compassionate, yet able to lead in strength.

D. DUTIES TO HANDLE THE NEEDS OF WOMEN:

A. Fellowship among the brethren. This calls for luncheons, breakfasts, Bible studies, etc.

B. Training programs to help women grow spiritually.

C. Reaching out to other women is an essential part of women's ministries.

E. LEADER OF THE WOMEN'S MINISTRY:

Their functions will be:

* They will act as a facilitator.

* They will come up with ideas and be a plan coordinator.

* They will set the agenda for meetings and events.

* They will moderate the discussions and through prayer and fellowship build a vital women's ministry.

* They will develop strategies and networking within the church and the community.

* They will create classes for the development of spiritual growth.

* They will create support groups for special needs programs.

Examples As Per Below:

* Single women

* Single women parenting

* Child abuse

* Stress management

* Self-improvement

* Empty-nest syndrome

* Elderly women

The Leader of the Women's Ministry must be able to bring women together for prayer meetings. She must be a team player, and be able to delegate. She must work for the good of women, so they can live a life dedicated to Jesus Christ.

F. SUMMARY:

The Women's Ministry Chairperson is involved in almost every dimension that is related to the Women's Ministry of the local church. If women are left out of the equation of service one half of the strength of the body is missing.

Being able to meet the growing challenges that women face today with being working mothers, single mothers and the stress of maintaining a balanced life the women's leader must, herself, walk a balanced Christian life with family, church, community and personal growth time.

It is a hard task, but because women are given, by God, gifts, talents and the ability to serve; women seem to have the capacity for great potential in the church.

Compassion, love, prayer, discipleship, fellowship and service are all elements the Women's Ministry Chairperson must excel in.

XI. CHURCH SECRETARY

SCRIPTURAL PURPOSE: 2 Samuel 8:17

"And Zadok the son of Ahitub, and Ahimelech the son of Abiathar, were the priests; and Seraiah was the scribe;"

A. ADMINISTRATIVE PURPOSE:

The Church Secretary holds a very powerful position of influence within the church hierarchy and must be a person of integrity and be an excellent communicator through writing, verbal and even computer skills.

The Church Secretary must have an ability to work independently and yet be submitted to the authority of the pastor without usurping his position. That is a difficult task; as it is a fine line sometimes. The secretary must have the interest of the church and the integrity of the church as the utmost priority.

The Church Secretary must have a professional image and represent the pastor in the city, state and congregation. They perform administrative and clerical duties and they must be an expert in the use of various office machines and equipment.

B. REQUIREMENTS:

They are responsible for day to day operations within the church structure.

They must be able to work independently and on-site supervision is not needed over them.

They must be computer literate: Microsoft ® Office Professional Edition, Microsoft Word, Access, Excel, Power Point, HTML and Outlook.

*They must be the liaison between management, congregation and pastor.

*They must assist in all the writing, editing, production and distribution of all church communication materials.

**They must handle all correspondence; telephone, facsimile, email and postal materials.

*They will be required to do a background check.

*They must be flexible and show a mature level of patience; as the typical church day can have situations that can be very stressful.

*They must be able to handle personal, confidential and non-confidential information in private and honorable ways.

*They must be able to do basic filing, typing and taking and transcribing dictation.

*They must be an expert in English, grammar, spelling, and math.

*They must be able to answer phones in a professional and interesting manner.

*They must take messages, screen calls, prioritize and remain polite and genuine in concern and interest.

*They will answer to the Senior Pastor.

 *They must be able to attend staff meetings, keep accurate records of corporate meetings and set up agendas and maintain copies of all church correspondence.

*They are responsible for the official documents of the corporation such as, the official seal, the bylaws and the minutes of meetings.

* They must understand the business of the church thoroughly.

*They must be able to supervise and coordinate the work.

*They must be a confident to the Pastor or Chief Executive Officer.

*They must be detail oriented.

*They must have the capacity to remain calm, at all times, no matter what situation.

*They must be sincere and loyal to the Lord, pastor and congregation.

***THE WORK TOOLS OF THE SECRETARY:
Provided By Church

* Assigned a church office space as their personal place of work.

* Assigned a specific desk.

* Assigned a specific computer and telephone.

C. DAILY BASIC RESPONSIBILITIES:

I. TO THE PASTOR:

A. Make appointments, keep pastor's calendar.

B. Handle all correspondence and mail.

C. Typing of all letters, notes, minutes, reports, bulletins, newsletters, etc.

D. Preparing all corporate materials and agenda for meetings.

E. Solve problems as relates to job operations.

F. Screen calls and visits.

G. Hold all conversations in private.

II. TO THE CONGREGATION:

A. Be a liaison between pastor, staff, and congregation.

B. Make sure all bulletins, newsletters or printed materials are available to the people.

D. SUMMARY:

The Church Secretary is such a focal point of communication between the body of Christ, the community and the leadership that it takes a very detail oriented and organized person to feel the shoes of this position.

The Church Secretary must be flexible, yet set the standard for the organizations public image. They must be a servant in heart, a laborer in spirit and the confident of the top hierarchy of the church.

The Church Secretary must also have incredible skills with computers and software, English, writing, editing, to name a few, and have a creative side that can meet the needs of the pastor quickly.

The Church Secretary must be a confident to the pastor, yet maintain a proper professional attitude and character. It is sometimes important that they take a position of warning to a pastor, but the secretary should never assume they have the responsibility to carry out any corrections without pastoral request. It is a very fine line to know what you have the liberty to do and what you should wait on before acting.

The Church Secretary has one of the most influential positions within the church, so they must be above reproach and have a love for God that secures their hearts to serve with loyalty and discretion.

XII. CHURCH CLERK

SCRIPTURAL PURPOSE: 2 Samuel 8:15,16

"And David reigned over all Israel; and David executed judgment and justice unto all his people. And Joab the son of Zeruiah was over the host; and Jehoshaphat the son of Ahilud was recorder;"

A. ADMINISTRATIVE PURPOSE:

The Church Clerk primary responsibility is to be the "record keeper." Another task they must be excellent at is to keep the membership roles of the church.

*The Church Clerk must track new members, members that have moved out of the church umbrella and basically, be aware of the movements (in a business sense) of the church body. PRIMARY RESPONSIBILITIES:

* They must prepare and, if necessary repair or rewrite the history records of the church.

* They must maintain and add to the church directory.

* They are responsible for storing the minutes of meetings and reports.

* They must manage the church letters, membership, transfers, baptisms, etc.

* They must realize that the pictures, history, bulletins, events, and activities of the church need to be recorded and preserved for the next generation.

B. GENERAL QUALIFICATIONS:

   1. They must be an exceptional organizer.

   2. They must be an incredible people person.

   3. They must have a good reputation and work well with others.

   4. They must understand the vision of the church, in order to document a correct history.

C. SUMMARY:

   The Church Clerk has an interesting position, in that; they are considered the keeper of the written records and life actions of the church. They are to understand the concept of safe record keeping.

This does not just mean in accuracy, but also in safe keeping such as, safes, fireproof boxes and proper storing procedures. They are instrumental in leaving to the next generation an accurate picture of the vision, ministry and accomplishments of the church.

XIII. CHURCH TREASURER

SCRIPTURAL PURPOSE: Luke 12:42-44

"And the Lord said, who then is that faithful and wise steward, whom his lord shall make ruler over his household, to give them their portion of meat in due season? Blessed is that servant, whom his lord when he cometh shall find so doing. Of a truth I say unto you, that he will make him ruler over all that he hath."

A. ADMINISTRATIVE PURPOSE:

The Church Treasurer is a position that is to be taken very seriously by the man or woman of God who fulfills the role, duty and responsibility of the financial accountability and stability of the church corporation, organization and body of believers.

The Church Treasurer duties and responsibilities will include the payment of all church invoices and expenditures, the complete and accurate accounting of all financial activity of the church; including all the record keeping and the ability to give account of the financial condition of the corporation, organization and body of Christ within a short period of notice. In essence, they are responsible for keeping the accounting and the records of the church's financial status.

B. PRIMARY RESPONSIBILITIES AND DUTIES:

The data entry and complete accurate accounting records of all the church operations. Each department within the church shall have accurate and legible accounting and shall insure that the financial accounts of the church are maintained in complete accuracy with a check and balance system. The maintenance of the accounting shall be done daily or on a weekly basis.

In order for the church to maintain a level of integrity they must make sure all payments of church operating expenses are paid in a timely and regular manner. They must be paid in accordance with the invoice and the church should have an impeccable reputation with all creditors.

They should maintain a monthly reconciliation of bank statements, investment reports and all manner of financial business as it pertains to the church.

If there is a Finance Committee or Board the Treasurer shall give timely reports, and only pay expenditures out as the Finance Committee approves.

Treasure shall provide a check list of all checks made for expenditures to the Committee or Board.

The Treasurer shall be available for all meetings called by the Pastor, Board, or Finance Committee.

All payrolls shall be completed and all data entered into an accounting program, such as Quicken, or manual accounting skills done daily and weekly. Preparation of all tax, health, insurance, W2 forms and year end tax requirements made in a professional and legal manner.

All forms, data entry, IRS requirements and all tax deposits for payroll or employee packages must be made in a timely and responsible manner for all employees, staff, leadership and/or any persons of concern; such as speakers or professionals needed on a consistent basis. Must prepare a once a year financial report for the congregation.

C. GENERAL QUALIFICATIONS:

1. A degree in accounting or a working knowledge of basic accounting principles with a minimum of three years experience.

2. Great organizational skills.

3. Privacy and confidentiality are an absolute must. An accountant must be a person that has a high level of integrity and is considered very trustworthy.

D. DUTIES OR DEPARTMENTS CREATED TO HANDLE THE ACCOUNTING NEEDS:

1. They must keep an accurate accounting of contributions.

2. They must cover all supervision of all financial data entry.

3. They must make preparation of all deposits, data entries and making of deposits.

4. They must maintain contribution records and mail statements on an annual basis.

5. They must maintain general operations and/or building funds for future use.

6. They must maintain records for stewardship campaigns.

7. They must perform any tasks requested by the Finance Committee, Pastor or Board.

D. SUMMARY:

The Accountant or Treasurer must be able to function in the primary performance of professional accounting standards. They should be able to apply theories, principles, examine and analyze all kinds of financial transactions. The Professional accountants must perform work that is very analytical in nature and to a great extent their job becomes advisory in function.

There are several accounting departments they must be knowledgeable in (accounts payable, receivables, investments, trusts and special projects). Accountants perform many duties and must assure the organization's accounting figures are accurate in the recording of the financial transactions. They must be able to interpret reports, statements and be able to make financial projections based on the information at hand.

An Accountant must be able to analyze financial transactions and have the ability to identify potential financial problems and must be able to suggest or recommend corrective measures. The accountant must have knowledge of governmental accounting methods, be able to process necessary administrative forms and supervise clerical record keeping assuring excellent quality control.

An accountant must be a person of high integrity and realize the importance of a privacy code of ethics concerning pastors, staff, board and congregation. All financial data must be treated with the utmost privacy and confidentiality.

XIV. TRUSTEE MINISTRY

SCRIPTURAL PURPOSE: Philippians 4:18

"But I have all, and abound; I am full, having received of Epaphroditus the things which were sent from you, an odour of a sweet smell, a sacrifice acceptable, well-pleasing to God."

A. ADMINISTRATIVE PURPOSE:

The Trustee is legally and spiritually responsible for everything that goes on in and outside the church pertaining to proper functioning practices. Epaphroditus was trusted (trustee) with the offering that had been raised for Paul, and it was his sole responsibility to make sure it got to Paul.

The Trustees must be completely surrendered to God in their life, the church leadership and church vision. Everything the church does or accomplishes must be examined, not in the light of men, but in the light of the Scriptures. In essence, a trustee is responsible for all the real and personal properties of the church.

The Trustee has authority and should be given the responsibility to properly follow the laws of the land and the laws of Scripture. A fantastic trustee will make sure the laws of the land and the laws of Scripture are partners in the growth of the church, not adversaries. They have a responsibility over the funds of the church and must maintain ethical and sound business principles.

B. PRIMARY RESPONSIBILITIES:

* They must see that the vision of the ministry is carried out by maintaining an annual budget and fulfilling the plans for the church; by being accountable to the laws of God and the laws of the land.

* They should oversee the planning stages of the church for three to seven year cycles.

* Using the Articles of Incorporation and the Bylaws they select and remove all officers and agents of the Corporation.

* They may borrow money and incur debt on behalf of the Corporation.

* They must be committed to the general welfare of the members they represent. This means it is their job to examine all agendas of the church and question anything they feel is out of order. They must be willing to answer the congregation's questions and take to heart the congregation's feelings. They represent the congregation in a protective capacity.

* They must attend all trustee meetings, pastoral and staff meetings, if needed.

* They must be sound in Word and doctrine.

C. GENERAL QUALIFICATIONS:

1. They must carry out the resolutions of the Corporation.

2. They must provide guidance to the business managers, accountants and pastoral staff.

3. They must be able to negotiate contracts provided for in the budget and approved by the congregation.

4. They must have a good reputation.

5. They must be committed to the vision of the church.

6. They must be a team player, as it pertains to the rest of the Board of Trustees.

7. They must participate in board appointed committees.

8. They must be an advisor to the pastor, staff and leadership of the church. They must also be

a communicator to the congregation, of the plans and budget of the church.

D. SUMMARY:

The Trustee holds a tremendous position of trust within the church. They are basically the interpreter of the law and church operations under the law, but based on a spiritual vision. They must make sure that the monies, accounts, organization and plans are carried out with the highest integrity and honesty. They are accountable for being honest in the operational process of ministry.

They must know the law, the Word and be corrective in any department of the church, if correction is needed. Some examples that show the office are:

***Romans 16: 23**, "Gaius mine host, and of the whole church, saluteth you. Erastus the chamberlain of the city saluteth you, and Quartus a brother."

***Ephesians 6:21-22** "But that ye also may know my affairs, and how I do, Tychicus, a beloved brother and faithful minister in the Lord, shall make known to you all things; Whom I have sent unto you for the same purpose, that ye might know our affairs, and that he might comfort your hearts."

XV. FINANCE SECRETARY

SCRIPTURAL PURPOSE: I Chronicles 28:1

"And David assembled all the princes of Israel, the princes of the tribes, and the captains of the companies that ministered to the king by course, and the captains over the thousands, and captains over the hundreds, and the stewards over all the substance and possession of the king, and of his sons, with the officers, and with the mighty men, and with all the valiant men, unto Jerusalem."

A. ADMINISTRATIVE PURPOSE:

A Finance Secretary has very viable and basic responsibilities. They are usually an elected officer of the Corporation. Their obligations to the Corporation are usually spelled out clearly in the bylaws of the Corporation.

They take care of the actual accountability for all receipts and accounting reports, as it pertains to the monies collected, received and disbursed by the Corporation.

B. PRIMARY RESPONSIBILITIES:

* They must check that all monies are accurately accounted for and being used as recorded.

* They must keep an accurate record in bound ledgers or software that is backed up that indicates dates of receipts and all receipts must be accounted for and numbered.

* They must keep track of any notes or disbursements that have been made by the Corporation.

* Using the Articles of Incorporation and the Bylaws they determine who shall be responsible, and when the monies received should be deposited.

* They prepare annual financial reports and submit all records for audits.

C. GENERAL QUALIFICATIONS:

1. They must be above average in math and should have an accounting degree.

2. If they have no accounting degree they should show strong administrative skills and organizational ability.

D. SUMMARY:

The Finance Secretary basically documents, for the organization, the money trail. They keep the day to day journal of the activities and decisions of the Corporation. Communication of day to day operations, preparation of needed documents, and fulfillment, in making sure records are handled and filed correctly, are the main functions of the Finance Secretary.

XVI. CHURCH SCHOOL SUPERINTENDENT

SCRIPTURAL PURPOSE: II Timothy 2:1, 2

"Thou therefore, my son, be strong in the grace that is in Christ Jesus. And the things that thou hast heard of me among many witnesses, the same commit thou to faithful men, who shall be able to teach others also."

A. ADMINISTRATIVE PURPOSE

The Church School Superintendent should have a general knowledge of education policies and procedures of the state in which the church is established. They must understand that the community has certain expectations for a good education for their children, and they should be a person of great leadership and communication skills.

The Church School Superintendent must be able to explain their standard of education to those concerned. They must be of excellent moral character and have a business mind in administration, curriculum, hiring and firing policies of teachers, a great supervisor and caretaker of the educational system they are placed in authority over.

The Church School Superintendent must understand state law and be able to follow state mandated requirements for evaluation tests, of comparisons, to other schools and states.

B. PRIMARY RESPONSIBILITIES AND DUTIES:

*They must understand that their job performance demands that they be the educational and business leader of the school.

*They must oversee, select, plan and evaluate the curriculum that will be used in the school.

*They must be an excellent long term and short term goal setter. They must be a great motivator in order for the goals to be successful.

*They must serve in the capacity of Chief Executive Officer of the Church School Steering Committee.

*They must keep current with laws, state and federal, and even trends in education.

*They must oversee and maintain a professional staff of teachers and essential job positions necessary for a successful school.

*They must ensure that all state and federal records are accurate, in order and filed on schedule.

* They must maintain a safe and learning school environment.

C. GENERAL QUALIFICATIONS:

1. A degree in Education

2. Great organizational skills.

3. Have a proven record in building a strong educational program.

D. DUTIES OR DEPARTMENTS CREATED TO HANDLE THE SCHOOLS NEEDS:

` 1. They must supervise custodial, maintenance, safety, transportation and all school programs which make for a normal school day's success.

2. They must supervise and manage all developments of a professional staff.

3. They must make sure an annual budget is prepared and met.

4. They must maintain accurately all school records, finances and student records.

5. They must have the power to direct spending and purchases as needed.

6. They must be able to advise the School Board of all procedures being used and substantiate them.

7. They must be able to keep current with educational thought and practices.

E. SUMMARY:

The Church School Superintendent is responsible for the effective operation of the school or educational institutions created by the church. They must be administrative, instructional and able to dispense intelligent and pertinent advice to the Church Steering Committee.

The Church School Superintendent must be an effective communicator and a liaison between the community, the families and the church board. Being able to understand the law and obey the law by creating policies and rules in alignment with the law are major responsibilities for the safeguarding of the students' welfare.

Note: This position is some churches is called, The Sunday School Superintendent!

XVII. CHRISTIAN EDUCATION DIRECTOR

SCRIPTURAL PURPOSE: Romans 12:3, 6, 7

"For I say through the grace given unto me, to every man that is among you, not to think of himself more highly than he ought to think; but to think soberly, according as God hath dealt to every man the measure of faith...Having then gifts differing according to the grace that is given to us, whether prophecy, let us prophesy according to the proportion of faith: Or ministry, let us wait on our ministering: or he that teacheth, on teaching;"

A. ADMINISTRATIVE PURPOSE:

The Education Director is a position that has a broad scope of duties attached to it. It is a position that must guide or help determine the policy of the educational program of the church and is in complete agreement with the pastor.

The Education Director must be a well-rounded individual, as they will have to determine the best curriculum and educational programs that are to be established within the church program.

The resources to be used in the programs must be examined, evaluated and chosen according to the ability of the education director's knowledge and understanding of all different levels of learning styles and abilities.

Last, but not least, they must also formulate a budget and educational plan, including the hiring of all staff positions within the educational process, for the church board to review and approve. This area of planning shall include short and long term goal setting, report writing and documenting the progress of the plans instituted.

B. PRIMARY RESPONSIBILITIES AND DUTIES:

*To develop and make sure the dates are implemented on an annual calendar for the educational activities and functions within the church.

* To keep a current knowledge of the new training and educational tools available. This will include attending conferences and seminars that are outside the time frame of the working hours.

*To maintain daily, weekly and monthly reports of students, programs, teachers, calendars and reports to pastor or governing board.

*To assess the needs of staff, students and congregation as it pertains to education and submit it to the pastor or board as to any recommendations and procedures that may need to be changed or added.

*To research different formats of curriculum; order, train and implement.

C. GENERAL QUALIFICATIONS:

1. A degree in Education or at least five years of educational experience.

2. Great organizational skills.

3. Teaching in classrooms or at church events if necessary.

4. Support and promote spiritual growth opportunities such as, camps, Bible studies, conferences, seminars and planned events of the church.

5. To be able to coordinate with other ministries, educational programs and staff.

6. To provide for a library and personnel to staff it.

7. To provide guidance and counsel for youth when needed.

D. DUTIES OR DEPARTMENTS CREATED TO HANDLE THE EDUCATIONAL NEEDS:

1. They must oversee teachers and staff committees.

2. They must be the person to "go to" when information is needed be clarified or learned about. They must be able to facilitate communication clearly.

3. They must work with a Sunday school staff of paid workers or volunteers.

4. They must maintain a library or an Internet library for use of students.

5. They must create an office for counsel and meetings of parents and students.

6. They must maintain general educational operations and facilitate reports as needed by the city, state, and federal government.

E. SUMMARY:

The Christian Education Chairperson or Director must be a person with a vision and who is enthusiastic, creative and has great faith. They must have love for children of all ages and in all circumstances.

The Christian Education Chairperson or Director must nurture the spiritual growth as well as the academic growth of children of all ages. One of the greatest characteristics this educational director must have is the ability to see the worth and dignity of every child.

The Christian Education Chairperson or Director must be highly organized and able to meet goals and obligations in a timely way and manner. They will work long, hard, tedious hours and they still must keep an enthusiastic spirit. Most of all they must be willing to serve God through their work with children of all ages.

XVIII. CHURCH CUSTODIAN

SCRIPTURAL PURPOSE: Exodus 35:30, 31; 36:1

"And Moses said unto the children of Israel, See, the Lord hath called by name Bezaleel the son of Uri, the son of Hur, of the tribe of Judah; And he hath filled him with the spirit of God, in wisdom, in understanding, and in knowledge, and in all manner of workmanship;"

"Then wrought Bezaleel and Ahboliab, and every wise hearted man, in whom the Lord put wisdom and understanding to know how to work all manner of work for the service of the sanctuary, according to all that the Lord had commanded.

A. ADMINISTRATIVE PURPOSE:

The person who will assume the position of custodian is accepting an extremely important role in the overall functioning of the Church. Although the main requirements of the custodian are the maintenance of the building, as the Church; it is much more than that. The custodian will be working with people from every area of the Church.

They should have a valuable knowledge in the technical and material needs of the Church. They must also be able to work with everyone including small children and the elderly! A spirit of Christian love is essential in this job.

He or she must exemplify a character of friendliness, kindness and helpfulness. Although an extensive list of job duties will be listed the custodian must be able to see what is needed before it becomes a problem or before anyone else sees it.

They must understand that their responsibilities have a spiritual aspect as well as a physical one. The job duties are divided into time frames. In essence, it thought that the custodian will assume the position as the "caretaker" of the Church building, inside and out. The custodian accepts the responsibility for the spiritual concern for the proper maintenance of the Church, the same as he would do with his own valuable possessions.

B. REQUIREMENTS:

1. Experienced and able to lift a minimum of 50 lbs, climb   step ladders and follow written instructions.

2. Experience and knowledge of HVAC and different mechanical functions of the church building, inside and outside.

3. Experience and knowledge dealing with contractors, vendors and professionals outside the church hierarchy.

4. They must be on call 24/7. This is due to the fact that the unforeseen happens and emergencies must be dealt with immediately.

5. They must have a basic knowledge of maintenance and repair skills, such as painting, carpentry, plumbing, electrical and knowledge of construction terms and skills.

6. They will be required to do a background check.

7. They will have knowledge of state requirements for a child safe building.

8. They must be able to take directions from a number of different individuals.

9. They must be able to determine priorities based on the needs of the congregation and be adaptable to quick changes.

10. They must be flexible. The nature of the church "caregiver" position is difficult to assign designated days, weeks and months of

responsibilities. A weekly hourly position will be created, but the custodian must be willing to be available at all times.

11. They must be able to prepare different meeting rooms as needed.

12. They will answer to the Senior Pastor and the Administrative Staff.

13. They must be able to attend staff meetings when asked to participate.

14. They must be able to maintain the security of the building.

15. They must develop and maintain schedules for custodial staff and volunteers.

16. They must be able to supervise and coordinate the work.

17. They must be willing to be on call for weekends in the case of funerals, weddings, special events and scheduled or unscheduled needs for use of the facility.

C. PRIMARY RESPONSIBILITIES AND DUTIES FOR SECURITY PURPOSES:

* Maintain the security of the building inside and outside. See that doors are locked, windows are locked, lights are out, except for security lights, and that no one is left in the building and sets the security alarm. Makes sure the alarms are tested regularly and repairs are repaired as necessary.

* Maintains the fire alarm and checks the provider to insure that the fire alarm remains in constant and in optimum working condition. Makes sure all fire extinguishers are up to date and code for the building specifications.

* Must report any signs of vandalism or misuse of the facilities to the pastor, board, or police.

* Maintain a child safe building.

E. ROUTINE CLEANING RESPONSIBILITIES

I. Inside

**SANCTUARY

A. Sweep and vacuum any carpets and flooring before and after church services.

B. Dust all ledges, surfaces, baseboards, ceiling fans, chairs or pews.

C. Empty trash cans, wastebaskets and pick up papers.

D. Clean and straighten the altar area.

E. Make sure all floral arrangements have fresh water and are placed correctly.

F. Spot clean walls and surfaces as they need it.

G. Maintain, set and control all heating and air conditioning.

**OFFICES

A. Sweep and vacuum any carpets and maintain floors.

B. Dust all ledges and other surfaces in the room.

C. Clean and dust the phones.

D. Empty all wastebaskets

F. Clean all windows.

G. Clean shades or blinds.

**HALLWAYS AND ENTRY

A. Sweep all halls and entry way with dust mop, vacuum and cleaning supplies.

B. Clean and disinfect drinking fountains.

C. Spot clean walls and baseboards.

D. Dust all ledges, tops of coat racks and miscellaneous furniture.

E. Clean any widows, glass and steel surroundings of doors.

F. Replace light fixtures.

G. Clean light fixtures.

**CLASSROOMS

A. Vacuum all carpeted areas and maintain clean floors.

B. Sweep tile floors and disinfect.

C. Empty wastebaskets.

D. Clean windows.

E. Clean shades or blinds.

F. Clean chalkboards and dust all ledges.

G. Disinfect tops of desks and chairs.

H. Empty all pencil sharpeners.

**RESTROOMS

A. Clean and disinfect sinks.

B. Clean and disinfect toilet bowls-seats, urinals and any plumbing pipes.

C. Empty all wastebaskets and disposable bins.

D. Check for full hand soaps, paper towels and tissue supplies.

E. Clean mirrors.

F. Mop and disinfect all tile floors.

G. Clean doors and partitions.

H. Check and replace deodorant plug-ins.

I. Spot clean walls and ceilings.

J. Replace any light bulbs.

K. Clean all baseboards.

L. Clean exteriors of all dispensers in the restrooms.

M. Check that all toilets, urinals, faucets and drains are working.

II. Outside

A. Maintain signs and bulletin boards.

B. Check shrubbery and trees.

C. Sweep and pick up any parking lot and lawn areas.

D. Hose down outside doors and any place cobwebs or trash would collect.

E. Water grass, trees and plants.

F. SUMMARY:

The Custodian must be able to function in the primary performance of professional cleaning, repair, maintenance and security standards. They should be able to organize crews, work with management, be flexible and understand the importance of being the "caretaker" of the house of God.

Professional Custodians must perform work that is very physical in nature. To a great extent their job becomes pivotal in preparing the church, so that people are ministered to; and the experience of going to church is one of pleasure and enjoyment.

The Custodian must have the ability to identify potential maintenance problems and must be able to suggest, recommend or be able to bring corrective measures. The position of Church Custodian is a full time assignment with regularly scheduled hours and workdays.

The Custodian is expected to be a committed Christian with the ability to maintain positive relationships with the congregation, as well as church staff. They must demonstrate initiative, a desire for excellence, flexibility, to respond to needs throughout the church properties and they must be physically fit and have a positive work ethic.

XIX. KITCHEN COMMITTEE CHAIRPERSON

SCRIPTURAL PURPOSE: Acts 2:41, 42

"Then they that gladly received his word were baptized: and the same day there were added unto them about three thousand souls. And thy continued steadfastly in the apostles' doctrine and fellowship, and in breaking of bread, and in prayers."

A. ADMINISTRATIVE PURPOSE:

The Kitchen Committee Chairperson has a job that is really seen, but not usually heard. They must maintain the kitchen facilities of the church.

The Kitchen Committee Chairperson must also plan, prepare and serve meals to the body of Christ for various purposes. One thing for sure their work is greatly appreciated and if done in an organized and excellent spirit can truly build the fellowship of the church into a powerful body of workers.

B. PRIMARY RESPONSIBILITIES AND DUTIES:

*They must maintain adequate supplies for a well stocked kitchen.

*They must prepare menus and meals for all functions of the church when asked to.

*They must be able to coordinate volunteers and delegate jobs within the kitchen and meal process, maintaining a high level of safety, health codes and cleanliness.

*They must establish policies and rules for kitchen workers including making sure all city health codes are being followed.

*They should be a person who understands budget and cost control.

C. GENERAL QUALIFICATIONS:

1. An excellent cook.

2. Great organizational skills.

3. A person who can work behind the scenes and not receive a great deal of verbal reinforcement.

D. DUTIES TO HANDLE THE NEEDS OF CHURCH FUNCTIONS:

A. They must be a person able to plan, budget and organize a kitchen team.

B. They must be a person who can think on their feet because not everything in a kitchen goes as planned. They must be able to improvise should something burn or come out wrong.

C. They must understand city laws and regulations for health codes.

E. SUMMARY:

The Kitchen Chairperson has a position of great importance in helping grow the fellowship and the love of the body of Christ within the church. Through good, healthy meals people come together to share and commit to each other. It is a hidden work usually, but one that everyone recognizes.

XX. FLORAL COMMITTEE CHAIRPERSON

SCRIPTURAL PURPOSE: Genesis 2: 8, 9

"And the Lord God planted a garden eastward in Eden; and there he put the man whom he had formed. And out of the ground made the Lord God to grow every tree that is pleasant to the sight, and good for food; the tree of life also in the midst of the garden, and the tree of knowledge of good and evil."

A. ADMINISTRATIVE PURPOSE:

The expression of beauty within the church can often be best displayed by floral decorations. Floral arrangements can be used as focal points around the pulpit, the guest table, as wedding decorations and for a multitude of other purposes. Floral leaders must have a creative sense of style and structure and must have an artist's eye for color and presentation.

B. PRIMARY RESPONSIBILITIES AND DUTIES:

They must understand the differences of flowers, seasons and how to present a message through design.

*They must prepare arrangements for all functions of the church when asked to.

*They must be able to coordinate volunteers and work with different committee chairpersons to achieve the desires of those needing their services.

*They must water and keep the arrangements in good visual order.

*They should be a person who understands budget and cost control.

C. GENERAL QUALIFICATIONS:

1. They must be very creative and have artistic skills.

2. They must have great organizational skills.

3. They must be a person who can work behind the scenes.

4. They must be a person who works well without a great deal of verbal reinforcement.

D. DUTIES TO HANDLE THE NEEDS OF CHURCH FUNCTIONS:

A. They must be a person able to plan, budget and organize arrangements.

E. SUMMARY:

The Floral Chairperson has a very creative position within the body of Christ. The beauty of the Lord is often referred to in Scripture through flowers.

For example, The Lily of the Valley, The Rose of Sharon and many others show clearly the love of Jesus. The Floral Chairperson has been given a wonderful opportunity to show the beauty of His holiness through their gift of the arrangement of nature.

XXI. USHER MINISTRY CHAIRPERSON/PRESIDENT

SCRIPTURAL PURPOSE: Psalms 84:10

"For a day in thy courts is better than a thousand. I had rather be a doorkeeper in the house of my God, than to dwell in the tents of wickedness."

ADMINISTRATIVE PURPOSE:

The Usher Chairperson/President is truly the right arm of fellowship to the body of Christ. They convey friendliness and hospitality to guests as well as fellow believers. They set the tone of the service by their love.

PRIMARY RESPONSIBILITIES AND DUTIES:

1. Greet, by name if possible, every person coming into worship.

2. Escort worshiper to seat.

3. Assist any disabled people.

4. Be alert for security reasons.

5. Collections of offerings.

6. Know where emergency defibrillator and fire extinguishers are.

7. Make sure everyone has a bulletin or papers needed

8. After Service: Keep pews or seats clean, gather up papers and any trash, clean water glasses per service, check lost and found for items.

10. Tidy up church and prepare for next service

11. Be at least 15 to 30 minutes early for every service.

12. Make sure guest room is taken care of and work closely with hospitality ministry.

13. Make available nametags for each usher.

14. Assign offering duties to ushers.

15. If during the service something irregular should happen handle it with common sense and tact.

GENERAL QUALIFICATIONS:

1. A genuine love and liking of people

2. Good communication skills

3. Organizational skills

4. Dependable and trustworthy

DUTIES OR DEPARTMENTS CREATED TO HANDLE THE USHER MINISTRY NEEDS:

1. To guide the work of the ministry with a one year commitment.

2. Create and participate in monthly usher meetings to help unify the ushers and create the fellowship needed to discuss problems and solutions.

3. Have training sessions to teach offering skills and communion skills.

4. Turn in the offerings to designated person.

A Usher's President/Chairperson is the first example of Jesus the people will see when they come into the sanctuary you must present yourself in absolute love and tactfulness.

XXII. EVANGELISM MINISTRY CHAIRPERSON/PRESIDENT

SCRIPTURAL PURPOSE: Matthew 28: 19, 20 (KJV)

"Go ye therefore, and teach all nations, baptizing them in the name of the Father, and of the Son, and of the Holy Ghost: Teaching them to observe all things whatsoever I have commanded you: and, lo I am with you always even unto the end of the world. A'-Men"

ADMINISTRATIVE PURPOSE:

The Evangelism Chairperson/President has probably one of the most sacred duties of the Church besides the Pastor. They are responsible for caring out the last commands of our Lord and Savior, Jesus Christ, to go to the world and make disciples.

PRIMARY RESPONSIBILITIES AND DUTIES:

*Establish a ministry that makes sure the congregation reaches out to people with the Good News of Jesus Christ.

*Establish a ministry that supports and serves families and individuals so that they can be transformed into the image of Christ.

*Establish a ministry that goes outside the four walls of the Church, to build the Church of God geographically around the world.

GENERAL QUALIFICATIONS:

1. Dependable and committed to Christ.

2. A heartfelt concern that others need to know Christ.

3. Research is a skill needed in order to make appropriate plans for the church.

4. Exceptional communication skills

6. Organizational skills are a must as well as planning and evaluation the skills of others.
7. An ability to "really listen" and communicate at the level a person can understand.

DUTIES OR DEPARTMENTS CREATED TO HANDLE THE EVANGELISM MINISTRY NEEDS:

1. To guide the work of the ministry with a one year commitment.

2. Participate in meetings of the Church Council and Committees representing

3. Evangelism hopes and responsibilities.

4. Be accountable with cost, receipts, records, and history of results.

5. Make sure that follow-up and needs are backed up effectively;

6. Be a liaison between the church congregants, pastors and leadership.

WHAT YOU ABSOLEUTELY MUST BELIEVE:

1. Jesus Christ is the Son of God and can and will save everyone that comes to Him.

2. The Bible is the Word of God and it is infallible.

3. The love of Jesus is unconditional.

XXIII. OUTREACH MINISTRY CHAIRPERSON/PRESIDENT

SCRIPTURAL PURPOSE: Luke 14: 23

"And the Lord said unto the servant, Go out into the highways and hedges, and compel them to come in, that my house may be filled."

ADMINISTRATIVE PURPOSE:

The Outreach Chairperson is a vital link between the community and the Church. The purpose of the Outreach program is to reach the lost, and help to serve their spiritual as well as their physical needs. At its very core is the foundation of teaching and equipping the saints to come to the knowledge of who God is and making them responsible Disciples of Christ.

PRIMARY RESPONSIBILITIES AND DUTIES:

1. Establish a ministry that breaks through to the community allowing the love of Jesus Christ to be seen and felt.

2. Establish a ministry that supports and serves families and individuals so that they can be transformed into the image of Christ

3. Establish a ministry that goes outside the four walls of the Church, but the emphasis is on teaching and establishing a healthy body of believers.

4. Establish a ministry that coordinates with the community for helps.

5. Maintain and oversee the appreciation of visitors by calling, e-mailing or letter writing.

6. Establish a ministry that coordinates with the Evangelism Ministry of the Church.

GENERAL QUALIFICATIONS:

1. A heart dedicated to the service of Christ and others

2. Great organizational skills

3. Outstanding verbal and social skills.

4. Privacy and confidentiality are an absolute must. The character of the man or woman must be one that has integrity and is considered trustworthy.

DUTIES OR DEPARTMENTS CREATED TO HANDLE THE OUTREACH NEEDS:

1. Must develop a solid financial foundation to be able to serve the community in a long term capacity.

2. Must maintain teaching and discipleship as a main priority to establish and eventually branch out to missions through the Evangelism Ministry.

3. Must prepare people in body, mind, and spirit to become fruitful in the ministry and expand their sights to Evangelism.

4. Fulfilled with the Holy Spirit.
(Acts 1:8- "But ye shall receive power, after that the Holy Ghost is come upon you: and ye shall be witnesses unto me both in Jerusalem, and in all Judaea, and in Samaria, and unto the uttermost part of the earth.")

5. Outreach is the first step on the ladder to truly reach the world through Evangelism.

XXIV. HOSPITALITY CHAIRPERSON/PRESIDENT

SCRIPTURAL PURPOSE: Romans 12: 10, 13

"Be kindly affectioned one to another with brotherly love; in honour preferring one another; distributing to the necessity of saints; given to hospitality."

ADMINISTRATIVE PURPOSE:

The **Hospitality President/Chairperson** is a position that becomes the heartbeat of the church. How healthy the Body of Christ is can often be seen in the way hospitality is given to its members and to others.

The duties and responsibilities will include keeping a current list of volunteers for help with all church functions. They should be excellent at e-mailing and calling skills.

PRIMARY RESPONSIBILITIES AND DUTIES:

1. Maintain an adequate supply of inventory supplies regarding food and drinks.

2. They must schedule and assign responsibilities to volunteers for each and every church event.

3. They should maintain a monthly small cash account that is reconciled every month with statements to be turned over to the accountant.

4. Be responsible and insure proper clean up and storage of supplies.

5. Coordinate with members regarding supplies, food and drink donations.

6. Use e-mail and calling to keep in touch with volunteers, message needs, and assign tasks.

GENERAL QUALIFICATIONS:

1. A calm and pleasant personality.

2. Great organizational skills

3. Outstanding verbal and social skills.

XXV. THE CHURCH MEMBERSHIP/DISCIPLESHIP

SCRIPTURAL PURPOSE: Romans 12: 1-4

"**I BESEECH** you therefore, brethren, by the mercies of God, that ye present your bodies a living sacrifice, holy, acceptable unto God, which is your reasonable service. And be not conformed to this world: but be ye transformed by the renewing of your mind, that ye may prove what is that good, and acceptable and perfect, will of God. For I say, through the grace given unto me, to every man that is among you, not to think of himself more highly than he ought to think: but to think soberly, according as God hath dealt to every man the measure of faith. For as we have many members in one body and all members have not the same office: So we, being many, are one body in Christ, and every one members one of another. "

ADMINISTRATIVE PURPOSE:

The most important purpose of the membership/discipleship, (the church affiliates) is to build the church into **'the glory'** that gives praise unto the Lord. The membership/discipleship is the **'church local'** and a part of the **'universal church of believers'**. There physical bodies are the **temples of the Lord** (Holy

Ghost) and what is say, what they do, what they express and how they live should always bring glory to God.

As part of the local and universal church the disciples must understand the importance of representing the Lord to the world. As the body of Christ, they must **show/have** the integrity, holiness, righteousness and character that exemplify the **HOLINESSS OF GOD**. Even though no part of **humanity** is righteous within its self; yet humanity should at all times should strive to do the right things, that is, be willfully committed not practice sin.

I Corinthians 3:6-8 "I have planted, Apollos watered; but God gave the increase. So then neither is he that planteth any thing, neither he that watereth; but God that giveth the increase. Now he that planteth and he that watereth are one: and every man shall receive his own reward according to his own labor.

PRIMARY RESPONSIBILITIES AND DUTIES:

1. **TO PRAY**

The first and foremost obligation of the believer is to **PRAY**. If every believer would take this command of Jesus literally the works of the Church would be so much easier. The ground will have been tilled and the word is ready to be planted into good soil and ready to bring forth a great harvest.

2. TO ATTEND CHURCH

St. Matthew 18:20 "For where two or three are gathered together in my name, there am I in the midst of them."

To fail to come together as a group of believes stops the Holy Spirit from enabling one to grow and most importantly hinder one from going out ministering to the needs of humanity. We are commanded to fellowship and come together. Worshipping and fellowshipping corporately is the time that believers can refresh themselves both physically and spiritually. In worship we lend ourselves to participating in prayer, communion and giving.

Once we become affiliate with a local church we're obligation by God and membership itself, to support that church with all seriousness and commitment. The local church does need disciples for which they can **only COUNT**, it needs people for which for which they can **COUNT ON.**

SUPPORT THE WORK OF THE MINISTRY

James 2:15-17 "If a brother or sister be naked, and destitute of daily food, and one of you say unto them, 'Depart in peace, be ye warmed and filled;' notwithstanding ye give them not those things which are needful to the body; what doth it profit? Even so faith, if it hath not works, is dead, being alone."

The Church has a serious work to do in this world. The Church is the light to world and salt to the earth. The Church is God's **eyes, hands, feet, ear, mouth and arms**—without these no effective ministry can be accomplished. Nothing gets done without commitment, responsibility, sacrifice and work done in love.

St. Luke 4:18-"The Spirit of the Lord is upon me, because he hath anointed me to **preach** the gospel to the poor; he hath sent me to **heal** the brokenhearted, to preach deliverance to the captives, and recovering of **sight** to the blind, to set at liberty them that are **bruised**, [19] To preach the acceptable year of the Lord.

Therefore, now that Jesus Christ is in heaven with God the Father, we (the believers) are the light to the world and salt to the earth. Because of this, we are told greater works shall you do than these, because I go unto my father.

TO SUPPORT THE WORK OF THE PASTOR

It is imperative that the membership support their pastor. This position appointed by God and those who sit in the pastor sit has been given a great command.

Acts 20: 28-"Take heed therefore unto yourselves, and to all the flock, over the which the Holy Ghost hath made you overseers, to feed the church of God, which he hath purchased with his own blood."

God has given a great charge to the pastor and it is vital that your support their needs in prayer, sacrifice, helps and giving. The bible teaches that laborers are worthy of their works and muzzle not the ox that works in the vineyard—**compensation your pastor well**! The membership must be the arms and the legs of leadership, so that the body can work together for the glory of God.

Never **negatively talk** about your pastor and never allow anyone else to do the same. The bible teaches us to **"touch not mine anointed and do my prophets not harm"**. It must be understood that no pastor is **'perfect'**, (without sin). Always pray that God will give your pastor the power to resist the temptations of sin.

MAKING ROOM FOR OTHERS IN THE HOUSE OF GOD

It is a wonderful thing to find a House of Worship and settle in for all the blessings and enjoyment that comes to each believer. There is a peace in the Lord's house that the world will never know. We do not sit in the pews just for personal comfort; we are called to take in the word and give it out; to bring others into the body of Jesus Christ.

OBEY THE WORD TAUGHT

Matthew 12:50 "For whosoever shall do the will of my father which is in heaven, the same is my brother, and sister, and mother."

Obedience is what makes the church a functioning and vital part of life. It creates the foundation for which to build and the security to know that what is built will stand the test of time. When we are not obedience to God's Word, The Holy Spirit and The Lord Jesus, we act just like a witch.

GO TO WORK IN MY VINEYARD

Galatians 6:10 "As we have therefore opportunity, let us do good unto all men, especially unto them who are of the household of faith."

By command the believer is to go into all the world and preaching the gospel to every creature. Not only are we to preach the gospel, we must teach, feed the hungry, clothe the naked, give sight to the blind, and visit those who are in the hospital and prison.

St. Matthew 28:18-19-"Go ye therefore, and teach all nations, baptizing them in the name of the Father, and of the Son, and of the Holy Ghost: Go ye therefore, and teach all nations, baptizing them in the name of the Father, and of the Son, and of the Holy Ghost:"

Acts 1:8-"But ye shall receive power, after that the Holy Ghost is come upon you: and ye shall be witnesses unto me both in Jerusalem, and in all Judaea, and in Samaria, and unto the uttermost part of the earth".

GENERAL QUALIFICATIONS:

1. **Salvation:** Romans 10:9 "That if thou shalt confess with they mouth the Lord Jesus, and shalt believe in thine heart that God hath raised

him from the dead, thou shalt be saved."

2. **Baptized**: Acts 2:38 "Then Peter said unto them Repent, and be baptized every one of you in the name of Jesus Christ for the remission of sins, and ye shall receive the gift of the Holy Ghost."

XXVI. CONCLUSION

In closing it has been a joy for me to research and formulate this information, of which, I believe will be an asset to you and your local church.

It is my prayer that you will continue to read other related materials which will better equip you to be a good leader and excellent follower of the Lord Jesus Christ.

It is when *"Leadership",* not just the pastor only, but all who serve in the role of ministering to others; know their positions and are well trained, that the ship will sail smoothly, even during turbulent times and difficult storms.

I have been blessed of God to have served over thirty (30) years ministering to the body of Christ and it has been a joy. It is very rewarding to see others grow in grace and in the knowledge of our Lord and Savior Jesus Christ.

The local church, in my opinion is the most important vehicle in the world. It is a fact that when all cylinders are properly serviced and every entity in their respected lane (ministry position)—the vehicle will performed at it optimum level.

So, make full proof of your ministry and do the work of a Christian—fight the good fight, keep the faith that you might finish your task and make full proof of your walk (ministry) in the Lord!

Joseph R. Rogers, Sr., D. Min.

A Co-Laborer In Kingdom Building

XXVII. Author's Contact Information & Other Works

Mailing Address:

1313 Ujamaa Drive, Raleigh, NC 27610

Phone Nos. (919) 208-0200, (919) 829-7179

Email Address:

jroger3420@aol.com,

Websites:

http://www.gpcminc.

Christian Discipleship And The Holy Spirit Study Series
Equipping For And Engaging
In Christian Warfare

Dr. Joseph R. Rogers Sr.

Sermon Series 13 (Sermons For All Occasions)
Sermon Outlines For Easy Preaching

Dr. Joseph R. Rogers Sr.

XXVIII. Notes

Notes, Con't.

Notes, Con't

CPSIA information can be obtained at www.ICGtesting.com
Printed in the USA
LVOW04s1325120115

422493LV00029B/343/P

9 781449 976637